LOOK

and

COOK

A COOKBOOK

for CHILDREN

TINA DAVIS

PUBLISHED IN 2004 BY STEWART, TABORI & CHANG
115 WEST 18TH STREET, NEW YORK, NY 10011
WWW.ABRAMSBOOKS.COM

CANADIAN DISTRIBUTION: CANADIAN MANDA GROUP
165 DUFFERIN STREET
TORONTO, ONTARIO M6K 3H6 CANADA

LIBRARY OF CONGRESS CATALOGING-IN-PUBLICATION DATA
IS ON FILE.
ISBN: 1-58479-358-9

EDITORIAL: LIANA FREDLEY AND BETH HUSEMAN
PRODUCTION: ALEXIS MENTOR AND KIM TYNER

THE TEXT OF THIS BOOK WAS COMPOSED IN SCALA
PRINTED IN THAILAND

5TH PRINTING

STEWART, TABORI & CHANG IS A SUBSIDIARY OF
LA MARTINIÈRE
GROUPE

This belongs to

STEWART TABORI & CHANG, NEW YORK

THIS BOOK IS

IN MEMORY OF MY GRANDMOTHER
Ida Jeger Davidovitz

DEDICATED TO MY MOTHER
Bernice Sapirstein Davis

AND FOR MY DAUGHTER
Lily Davis Snyder

ALL THE RECIPES IN THIS BOOK SHOULD BE MADE WITH THE ASSISTANCE AND SUPERVISION OF AN ADULT. COOKING IS FUN, BUT SAFETY COMES FIRST.

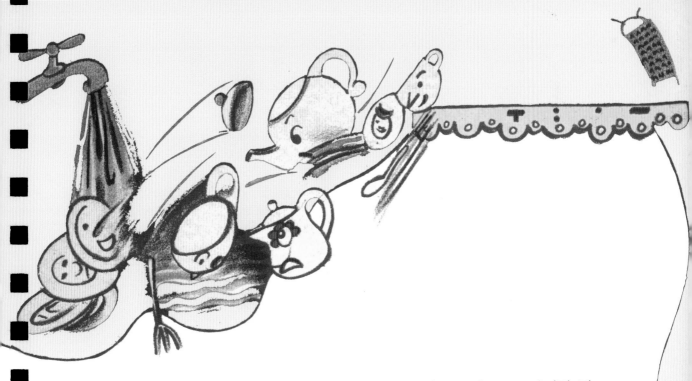

THE BEST MEAL I EVER ATE

The best meal I ever ate is one I ate often. It was made by my mother for my school lunch. Most days I had the same lunch as my classmates, but sometimes my mother would put a hot dog in my thermos, cover it with boiling water, and screw the cap on tight. She spread mustard on a hot dog bun, wrapped it in waxed paper, and put everything in my lunch box. At lunchtime, I opened the thermos, took out the amazingly hot hot dog, and put it on the bun. I was always the envy of everyone around me. Other times she made my sandwiches on pieces of frozen bread so that by the time I ate them, the bread had thawed and was very soft. But these sandwiches weren't nearly as good or amazing as the hot dog.

CONTENTS

KITCHEN
TOOLS

KITCHEN EQUIPMENT

APPLE CORER

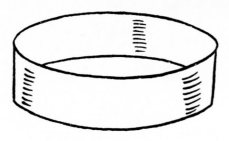

BAKING PAN

BUTTER KNIFE

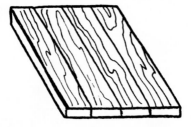

BREAD BOARD

CAN OPENER

CASSEROLE

CHOPPING KNIFE

CLOCK

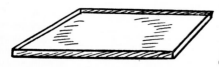

COOKIE SHEET

COOLING RACK

MEASURING SPOONS

MIXING BOWLS

MUFFIN PAN

PANCAKE TURNER

PARING KNIFE

POT HOLDERS

POTS

POTATO MASHER

SAUCEPANS

SHALLOW PAN

SLICING KNIFE

BISCUIT CUTTER

KETTLE

RING MOLD

BREAD KNIFE

LAYER CAKE PAN

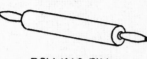

ROLLING PIN

CAKE RACK

LOAF CAKE PAN

ROTARY BEATER

(DOVER EGG BEATER)

CAKE TESTER

LONG-HANDLED SPOON

RUBBER CAKE SCRAPER

CANDY THERMOMETER

MEASURING CUPS

SAUCE PAN

CHOPPING KNIFE

MEASURING SPOONS

SIEVE (STRAINER)

COLANDER

MEAT RACK (TRIVET)

SKEWERS

ICE TRAY   CASSEROLE

STRAINER   WOODEN FORK

DOUBLE BOILER   WOODEN SPOON

APPLE CORER   WOODEN BOWL

GRATER   PARING KNIFE

PANCAKE TURNER   COLANDER

GRIDDLE   SAUCEPANS

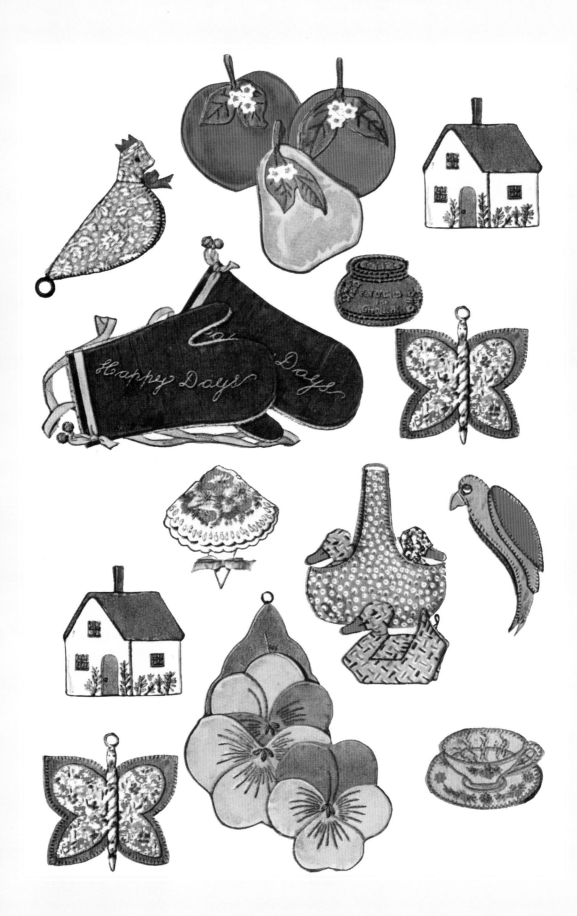

HOW TO MEASURE

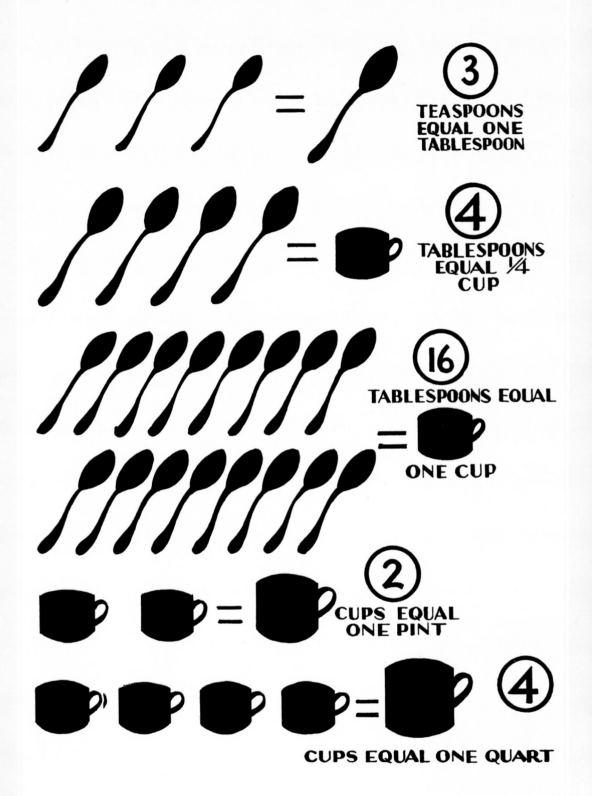

3 TEASPOONS EQUAL ONE TABLESPOON

4 TABLESPOONS EQUAL ¼ CUP

16 TABLESPOONS EQUAL ONE CUP

2 CUPS EQUAL ONE PINT

4 CUPS EQUAL ONE QUART

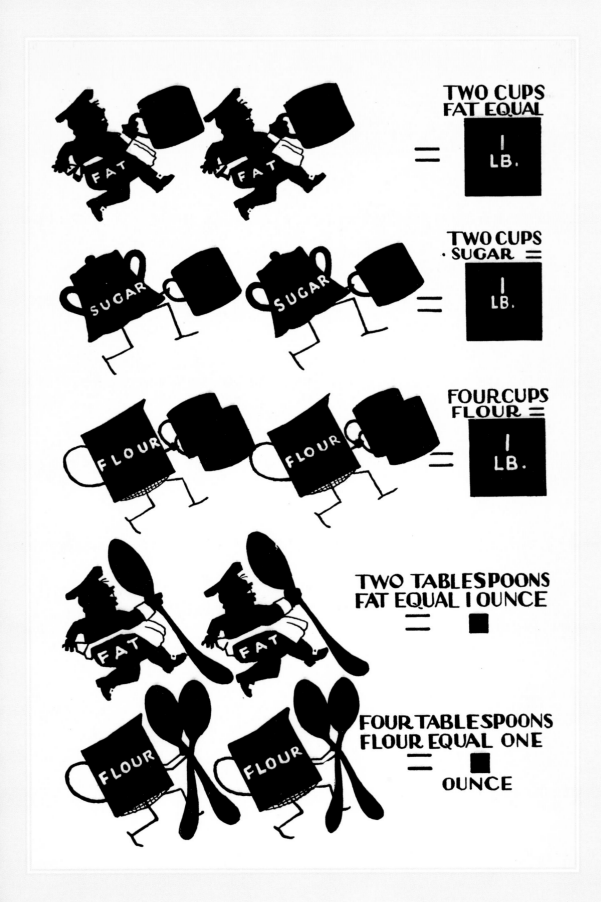

TWO CUPS FAT EQUAL = 1 LB.

TWO CUPS SUGAR = 1 LB.

FOUR CUPS FLOUR = 1 LB.

TWO TABLESPOONS FAT EQUAL 1 OUNCE = ■

FOUR TABLESPOONS FLOUR EQUAL ONE = ■ OUNCE

WHAT WE NEED TO KNOW ABOUT MEASURING

1. Measure all ingredients accurately. Measure dry ingredients first, then liquids, then fats.

2. Use wooden forks and spoons for stirring and mixing.

3. Use standard measuring cups and spoons. All measurements are level so use a knife to push off extra amount.

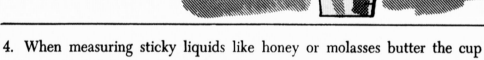

4. When measuring sticky liquids like honey or molasses butter the cup or spoon lightly so syrup will pour out easily.

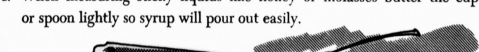

5. When measuring fats, pack solidly into cup or spoon and level off with knife.

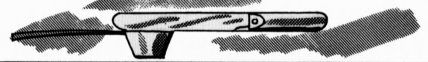

6. When measuring flour,

always sift flour first then measure it.

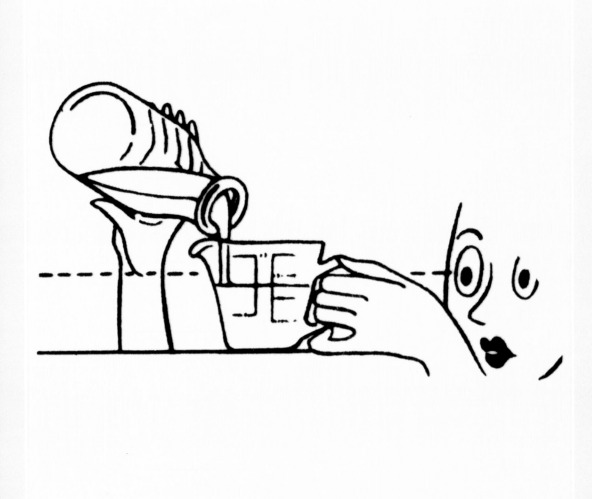

SAFETY FIRST

Always cook with an adult.

Wash and dry your hands before you start. Always make sure your hands are completely dry before using any electrical appliance.

Wear an apron, roll up your sleeves, and tie your hair back if it is long.

Use potholders when touching handles of pots on the stove and when removing pans from the oven. Always turn the handles of the pots toward the back of the stove. Do not leave the kitchen when the stove is on.

Ask an adult to help you use sharp knives. When you use a vegetable peeler, peel away from you.

Do not use your finger to taste something that is cooking. Use a spoon and take a bit of what you're cooking, let it cool, then sample it.

If you spill something on the floor, wipe it up right away so that someone doesn't slip and fall.

Never stand on a chair to reach the stove. Always have an adult help you.

Always turn off the stove and oven and clean up the kitchen after you are finished cooking.

RECIPES FOR ALL GOOD COOKS

1. Read the recipe *first*.
2. Get out all the things for the recipe (my older sister calls them "ingredients"). Get out the utensils you'll need — the pans, and spoons and so on.
3. Measure carefully. That way the recipes turn out right *every* time.
4. Do everything *just like the recipe says* to do it.
5. Clean up the kitchen so that you can cook again.

SAFETY IN THE KITCHEN

DON'T ever grab a pot handle on the stove with your hands. Use a pot-holder.

DON'T ever turn the handles of pots or frying pans outward so you'll bump into them. Always turn the handle away from where you walk.

SOUPS

SPLIT PEA SOUP

2 cups (about 1 pound) split green
  peas

2 tablespoons butter

1 cup carrots, *chopped*

1 cup onions, *chopped*

1 cup celery, *chopped*

8 cups water

1 tablespoon fresh thyme, or
  1 teaspoon dried

1 bay leaf

1 teaspoon sugar

2 teaspoons salt, or to taste

ground black pepper to taste

Rinse and pick over the split peas, discarding any debris. In a large soup pot, melt the butter over medium heat. Add the carrots, onions, and celery and cook for about 10 minutes, until soft. Add the split peas, 8 cups water, the thyme, and bay leaf and bring to a boil; lower the heat to maintain a simmer and cover the pot. Simmer, stirring occasionally to make sure the soup isn't sticking to the bottom of the pot, for about 1 hour, until the split peas are falling apart. Add the sugar, salt, and pepper and remove from the heat. Remove and discard the bay leaf. Let the soup cool for a few minutes before using the blender. Working in batches, carefully ladle it into a food processor or blender and purée until smooth. Return the soup to a clean saucepan and heat through, adding more water if the soup seems too thick. Serve very hot.

Serves 8 to 10.

VEGETABLE SOUP

2 tablespoons olive oil

½ cup onions, *diced*

½ cup carrots, *diced*

½ cup celery, *diced*

1 clove garlic, *minced*

1 cup potato, *diced*

½ cup green beans, *chopped into*
   1-inch pieces

½ cup peas, fresh or frozen

1 cup crushed canned tomatoes

1 bay leaf

1 teaspoon salt, or to taste

¼ teaspoon sugar, or to taste

¼ teaspoon ground black pepper, or
   to taste

¼ cup parsley, *chopped*

In a large pot, heat the oil over medium heat, then add the onion, carrot, celery, and garlic. Cook for about 10 minutes, stirring occasionally, until the vegetables are slightly softened but not browned. Add 4 cups water, the tomatoes, potato, green beans, and bay leaf. Bring to a boil, then lower the heat and simmer for 30 to 40 minutes, until the vegetables are tender but still hold their shape; about 5 minutes before the cooking time is up, add the peas. Season with salt, pepper, and sugar; taste and adjust the seasonings if necessary. Add the parsley just before serving. Serve hot.

Makes about 7 cups soup; serves 4.

CREAM OF TOMATO SOUP

½ teaspoon baking soda

1 (28-ounce) can tomato purée
   (about 3 cups)

2 tablespoons butter

1 small onion, *finely chopped*

1½ cups milk

1½ cups light cream

1 bay leaf

1 teaspoon salt

¾ teaspoon sugar

Stir the baking soda into the tomato purée and set aside (this will prevent the soup from curdling when you add the tomatoes to the milk and cream). The mixture will bubble up a bit, but this is okay.

In a large pot, melt the butter over medium heat; add the onion and cook until just softened, about 2 minutes. Add the milk, cream, and bay leaf and stir to combine. When the mixture is warm, add the tomato mixture, salt, and sugar. Bring the soup just to a boil, then immediately remove from the heat. Taste and add more salt and sugar if necessary; remove and discard the bay leaf. Serve hot. Makes about 6 cups soup; serves 4 to 6.

CHICKEN NOODLE SOUP

¼ pound (4 ounces) egg noodles, uncooked

4 cups chicken broth, canned or homemade

½ cup peas, fresh or frozen

½ cup (about 2 stalks) celery, *sliced*

½ cup (about 2) carrots, *sliced*

2 cups chicken, *cooked and shredded*

1 tablespoon fresh dill, *chopped*

¼ cup parsley, *chopped*

salt and pepper to taste

Cook noodles according to the directions on page 75. Drain and set aside. Place chicken broth in a large pot over high heat and bring to a boil. Add peas, celery, and carrots. Simmer, covered, for about 10 minutes, or until the vegetables are tender. Add the chicken and the drained noodles. Stir in the dill and parsley just before serving. Serve hot.

Serves 4 to 6.

MAIN DISHES

TUNA NOODLE CASSEROLE

1 (10¾-ounce) can condensed
   cream of mushroom soup

½ cup milk

2 (6-ounce) cans tuna,
   drained and flaked

1 cup frozen baby peas

¼ cup red bell pepper, *diced*

3 cups cooked pasta (such as elbow
   macaroni, or egg noodles; see note)

½ cup breadcrumbs mixed with
   2 tablespoons melted butter, or ½
   cup potato chips, *crushed*

Preheat the oven to 400°F. In a 9-by-12-inch baking dish, combine the soup, milk, tuna, peas, bell pepper, and pasta. Bake for 20 minutes. Remove from the oven and stir the mixture thoroughly. Top with the breadcrumbs and butter, return the dish to the oven, and bake for about 15 minutes longer, until the topping is nicely browned and the casserole is bubbling around the edge of the dish. Serve hot. Serves 4.

Note: Eight ounces dried pasta will yield about 3 cups cooked; see How to Cook Pasta (page 75).

MEATLOAF

1 small onion, *diced*

1 clove garlic, *minced*

1 tablespoon butter, plus more for
  the pan

1½ pounds ground beef

¾ cup bread crumbs

1 egg

1 tablespoon brown sugar

¼ cup tomato ketchup

½ teaspoon salt

¼ teaspoon ground black pepper

Preheat the oven to 350°F. Butter a 9-by-5-by-3-inch loaf pan. In a small frying pan over medium heat, cook the onion and garlic in the butter until golden and soft but not browned, about 6 minutes. Transfer the mixture to a large bowl and add all the remaining ingredients. Mix well with a large fork or your hands, then turn the mixture out into the prepared loaf pan and pat the top smooth. Bake for 1 hour. Remove the pan from the oven and let the meatloaf rest for 10 minutes before slicing, otherwise it will fall apart. Serve hot.

Serves 6.

You will need to make three recipes for S P A G H E T T I A N D M E A T -
B A L L S . *You can make the meatballs and the sauce up to a day in advance;
refrigerate them, covered, separately. When ready to serve, combine the meatballs and
sauce in a pot and simmer them together for at least 10 minutes, while you cook
the spaghetti.*

SPAGHETTI AND MEATBALLS

TOMATO SAUCE

2 tablespoons oil, vegetable or olive

1 small onion, *finely diced*

1 clove garlic, *minced*

1 (28-ounce) can crushed tomatoes,
   including juice

1 teaspoon salt

½ teaspoon sugar

1 teaspoon dried oregano

4 tablespoons tomato paste

2 tablespoons butter

Place the oil in a pot over medium heat. Add the onion and garlic and sauté until soft but not browned, about 5 minutes. Add all the remaining ingredients except the butter and bring to boil. Lower the heat and simmer for 10 minutes. Add the butter and simmer 5 more minutes. Set aside until you're ready to add the meatballs.

TURN THE PAGE FOR THE
MEATBALL RECIPE

SEE PAGE 75 FOR
HOW TO COOK PASTA

MEATBALLS

1 pound ground beef

¾ cup breadcrumbs

1 egg, *lightly beaten*

1 small onion, *finely chopped*

1 clove garlic, *minced*

3 tablespoons parsley, *chopped*

1 teaspoon dried oregano

1 teaspoon salt

¼ teaspoon ground pepper

2 tablespoons olive *or* vegetable oil

Combine all the ingredients except the oil in a large bowl and mix well (it's easiest to use your hands for this). Form the mixture into about sixteen 1½-inch balls. Heat half of the oil in a large frying pan over medium-high heat and add half of the meatballs. Cook for 8 to 10 minutes, turning every few minutes, until well browned on all sides. Remove the meatballs to a plate. Add the remaining oil and the remaining meatballs to the pan and cook until browned.

Putting it all together: Taste the sauce to see if it needs more salt, then add the meatballs. Simmer the sauce for with the meatballs for 10 minutes and keep it warm.

Meanwhile, cook the pasta in a large pot of boiling salted water following the directions in HOW TO COOK PASTA *(page 75). Serve the pasta with the sauce and meatballs spooned over the top.*

Serves 4.

He-Man Hamburgers

1 pound ground beef

¼ cup onion, *finely chopped*

1 egg yolk

½ teaspoon salt

¼ teaspoon pepper

The secret to juicy and tender hamburgers is to handle the meat as little as possible. The more you squeeze the meat, the tougher it becomes. In a large bowl mix together all the ingredients. A good way to do this is to use two forks, as if you are tossing a salad. Divide the mixture into 4 portions, and using your hands, gently shape into 4 patties about ¾-inch thick.

Heat a frying pan over medium-high heat until it is very hot. Place the patties in the pan and cook for about 5 minutes, or until the bottoms are nicely browned. Turn and cook on the other side for 3 to 4 minutes or until done the way you like them—check the doneness with the tip of a knife if necessary. Serve the burgers just as they are or on a toasted bun with a slice of tomato, a slice of onion, a slice of cheese, and a leaf of lettuce. However you serve it, don't forget the ketchup!

Serves 4.

These are the tins all labelled and stacked, filled with the fish so tightly packed, all from the boats that lower the nets, that catch the shining salmon.

This is Amelia, caught in the act, of eating the salmon so tightly packed, all from the boats that lower the nets, that catch the shining salmon.

SALMON PATTIES

1 small onion, *diced*

1 tablespoon butter

2 (7½-ounce) cans salmon,
    drained, flaked, bones and dark
    skin removed

2 eggs, *beaten*

1 cup breadcrumbs

¼ cup parsley, *chopped*

salt and pepper, to taste

2 tablespoons oil

In a small frying pan over medium heat, cook the onion in the butter until soft but not browned, about 6 minutes; remove from the heat. Transfer the onion to a large bowl and let cool completely, then add the salmon, eggs, breadcrumbs, parsley, salt, and pepper. Mix well, and use your hands to shape the mixture into 4 to 6 patties about ½-inch thick.

Heat the oil in a large frying pan over medium heat. Add the patties and cook until browned on one side, about 5 minutes, then carefully turn the patties over and cook the other side for about 5 minutes until browned. Serve hot.

It is customary to serve these with peas (simply boil frozen peas for a few minutes in a saucepan on the stovetop) and mashed potatoes (see page 54). But you can also serve them like burgers on a bun with lettuce, tomato, and mayonnaise. You can also substitute tuna for the salmon.

Makes 4 to 6 patties.

MACARONI AND CHEESE

BAKED

8 ounces elbow macaroni, uncooked

4 tablespoons butter

2 tablepoons flour

3 cups milk

1½ cups cheddar cheese, *grated*

1 teaspoon salt

½ cup breadcrumbs

2 tablespoons butter

Preheat the oven to 350°F. Cook the macaroni as described on page 75 and set aside.

In a large saucepan, melt the butter. Add the flour and stir until it is completely blended and slightly thickened. Add the milk and salt and bring just to a boil. Lower the heat and simmer for 1 to 2 minutes until the milk mixture begins to thicken, being careful not to overcook or the mixture will curdle. Add the cheese, and stir until the cheese has completely melted. Add the cooked macaroni and stir again. Pour into a greased 9-by-12-inch baking dish. Sprinkle the top evenly with the buttered breadcrumbs. Bake for 30 minutes until the cheese sauce is bubbling around the edges of the dish and the breadcrumbs are lightly browned. Serve hot. Serves 4.

MACARONI AND CHEESE

STOVETOP

4 tablespoons butter

2 tablespoons flour

3 cups milk

8 ounces elbow macaroni, uncooked

1 teaspoon salt

1½ cups cheddar cheese, *grated*

In a large saucepan melt the butter. Add the flour and stir. Cook for about 1 minute until mixture is completely blended and slightly thickened. Add the milk, macaroni, and salt. Stir together and bring just to a boil, being careful not to overcook or the mixture will curdle. Lower the heat, cover and simmer for 15 minutes or until the macaroni is tender, stirring occasionally so macaroni doesn't stick to the bottom of the pan. When macaroni is done, stir in cheese until melted, about 2 minutes.
Serves 4.

If you have the time, the baked version of this dish is more flavorful. But sometimes, when you're really hungry, faster is better.

BEANS AND FRANKS

1 (28-ounce) can baked beans

¼ cup onion, *minced*

2 tablespoons ketchup

1 teaspoon dry mustard

2 tablespoons brown sugar

6 hot dogs

Preheat oven to 350°F. In a mixing bowl combine the beans, onion, ketchup, mustard, and brown sugar. Slice the hot dogs into bite-size pieces. Pour half the bean mixture into a 1½ quart casserole. Place the hot dogs on top of the beans, then cover with the remaining bean mixture. Bake for 45 minutes, or until the beans are bubbling.

Serves 4 to 6.

PIGS IN BLANKETS

1 recipe MILE-HIGH BISCUITS (see page 68)

8 hot dogs

2 tablespoons butter, *melted*

Preheat the oven to 425°F. Roll the biscuit dough out into a rectangle about 10 by 18 inches, and about ¼-inch thick. Cut into 8 rectangles about 3 by 4 inches. Don't worry about exact measurements. Place a hot dog on the short edge of each rectangle and roll it up (the ends of the hot dogs will hang out), pinching the edges together. Place on a baking sheet, seam side down, and brush with the butter. Bake for about 40 minutes, until nicely browned.

Makes 8; serves 4.

VEGETABLES

MASHED POTATOES

2½ pounds potatoes (about 6
   medium), *peeled and cut into*
   quarters

4 tablespoons butter

½ cup milk

salt and pepper to taste

Place the potatoes in a large saucepan and add water to cover them by at least 1 inch.
Bring to a boil over high heat, then lower the heat and simmer for 25 to 30 minutes,
until the potatoes are soft when pierced with the tip of a knife but not falling apart.

Meanwhile, heat the butter and milk together in a small saucepan; do not let the
mixture boil. Set it aside. Place a large colander in the sink. Very carefully carry the
potato pot to the sink and slowly pour the water and potatoes into the colander and let
the potatoes drain. Return them to the pot over low heat. Using a potato masher, mash
the potatoes until smooth. Add the butter and milk mixture and beat with a wooden
spoon or a handheld electric mixer until fluffy. Add the salt and pepper and serve hot.
Serves 6.

SCALLOPED POTATOES

3 pounds (about 7 medium)
  potatoes

2 tablespoons flour

4 tablespoons butter, *diced,*
  plus more for greasing the dish

2 cups milk

1 teaspoon salt

½ teaspoon ground black pepper

½ cup firm cheese, such as cheddar
  or Gruyère, *grated* (optional)

Preheat the oven to 375° F. Grease an 9-by-12-inch baking dish. Peel the potatoes and slice them ¼-inch thick. Place half the potatoes in the baking dish. Add half the cheese if you are using it. Sprinkle with 1 tablespoon flour, 2 tablespoons butter, and ½ teaspoon salt. Add the remaining potatoes and sprinkle them with the remaining flour, butter, salt, pepper, and cheese if you are using it. Pour the milk over everything.

Cover with foil and bake for 45 minutes. Remove the foil and bake for 40 minutes longer. Serve hot.

PIG IN A POKE

1 large baking potato for every person

1 wiener for every person

butter or vegetable oil

Preheat the oven to 400° F. Using a brush, thoroughly scrub the potatoes; pat them dry and rub them lightly with the oil. Place on a baking sheet and bake for 40 to 45 minutes; remove from the oven, but leave the oven on. Holding a potato in your hand with a towel, use an apple corer or a dull knife to carefully make a hole lengthwise through the potato. Insert a wiener into the cavity. Repeat with the remaining potatoes and return them to the oven; bake for 15 minutes, or until the potatoes are soft and the wiener is heated through. Serve immediately.

~Insert wieners in holes, and finish baking ~~~

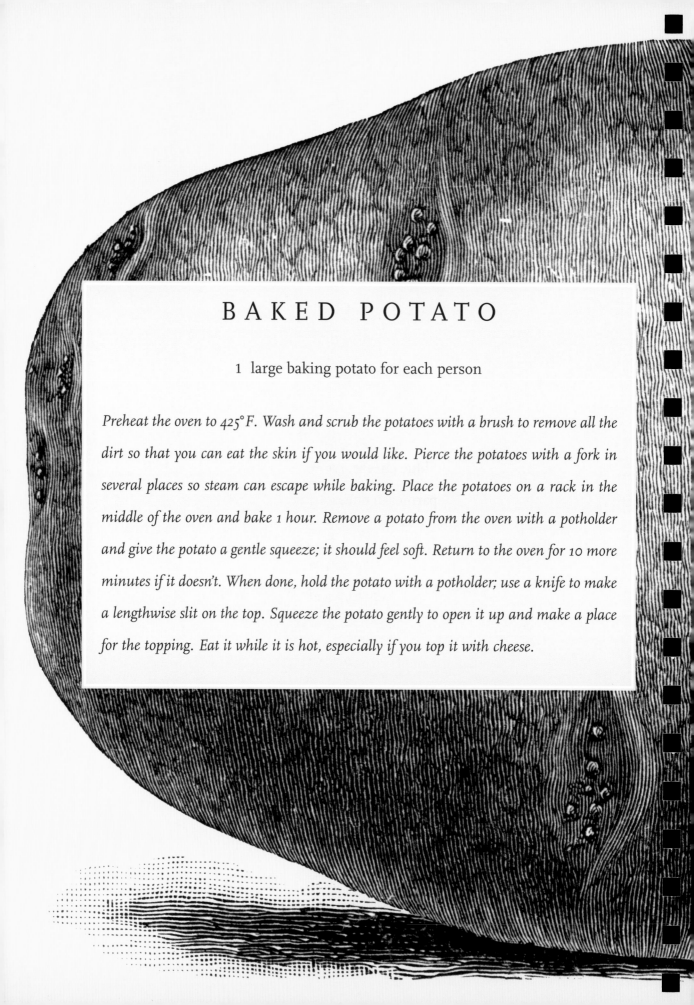

BAKED POTATO

1 large baking potato for each person

Preheat the oven to 425°F. Wash and scrub the potatoes with a brush to remove all the dirt so that you can eat the skin if you would like. Pierce the potatoes with a fork in several places so steam can escape while baking. Place the potatoes on a rack in the middle of the oven and bake 1 hour. Remove a potato from the oven with a potholder and give the potato a gentle squeeze; it should feel soft. Return to the oven for 10 more minutes if it doesn't. When done, hold the potato with a potholder; use a knife to make a lengthwise slit on the top. Squeeze the potato gently to open it up and make a place for the topping. Eat it while it is hot, especially if you top it with cheese.

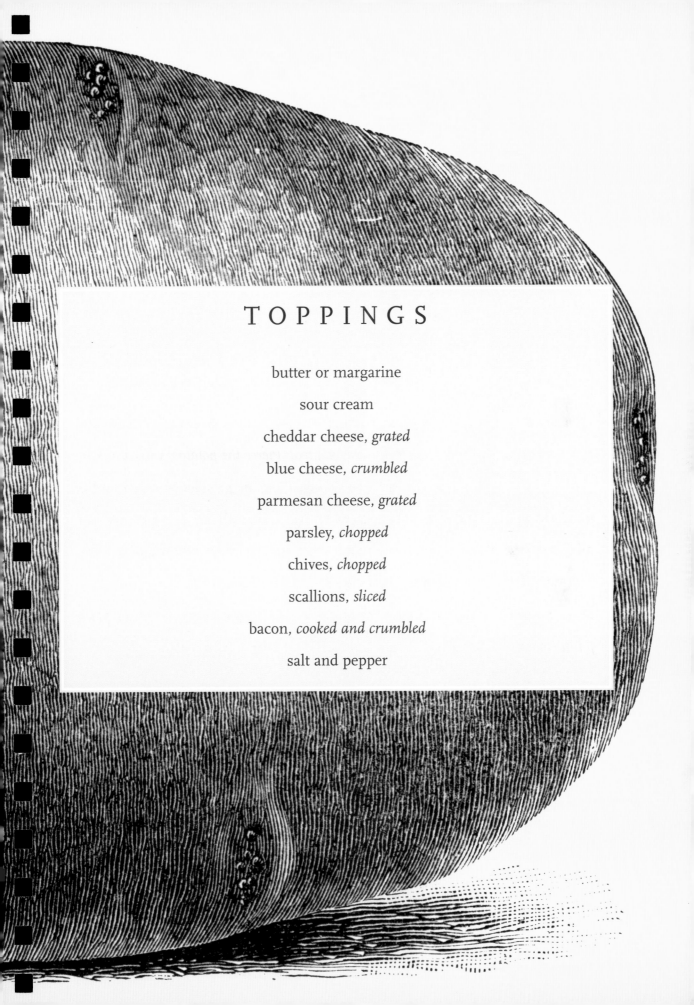

TOPPINGS

butter or margarine

sour cream

cheddar cheese, *grated*

blue cheese, *crumbled*

parmesan cheese, *grated*

parsley, *chopped*

chives, *chopped*

scallions, *sliced*

bacon, *cooked and crumbled*

salt and pepper

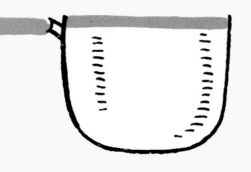

LARGE POT

TONGS

4 EARS CORN

BUTTER

SALT AND PEPPER

CORN ON THE COB

1 or 2 ears of corn for each person

butter, for serving

salt and pepper, for serving

Shuck the corn and remove the silks. Fill a large pot with 8 cups of water and bring to a boil. When the water is at a full boil, use metal tongs to gently place the corn into the water, one ear at a time. Boil for 2 to 5 minutes. The fresher the corn, the less time it needs to be cooked. Remove the corn from the water with tongs. Place on a platter and remove excess water by blotting with a clean dish towel or paper towel. Serve immediately with butter, salt, and pepper.

HOW TO COOK VEGETABLES

There are three basic ways to cook vegetables on the stovetop: boiling, steaming, or sautéing. Some vegetables are best suited to one method or another, and others can be cooked by any method. The secret to cooking vegetables is not to overcook them. They lose flavor, color, and nutrients when cooked too long.

TO BOIL: *Put 2 cups water in a 2-quart saucepan and bring to a boil. Gently slide about 2 cups vegetables into the water. The water should cover the vegetables by at least 1 inch. Bring back to a boil, then lower the heat and simmer. After 5 minutes, use the tip of a knife to check for doneness: the knife should slide in and out easily. When the vegetables are tender, lift out of the water with a slotted spoon and place in a colander which you have put in the sink. Let the vegetables drain, then serve hot.*

TO STEAM: *Place a steamer basket or metal colander in a pot with a lid. Add enough water to just touch the bottom of the steamer. Bring the water to a boil and slide the prepared vegetables into the steamer basket. Put the lid on the pot. Let the vegetables steam for 5 minutes, then use the tip of a knife to check for doneness: the knife should slide in and out easily. Steaming sometimes takes a little longer than boiling. When the vegetables are tender, use potholders to lift the steamer basket out of the water and let the vegetables drain in the sink. Serve while hot.*

TO SAUTÉ: *Place a small quantity of butter or oil in a fry pan big enough to hold the vegetables without crowding. Cook over medium heat, stirring often until tender. After 5 minutes, use the tip of a knife to check for doneness: the knife should slide in and out easily. You can serve the vegetables right from the pan.*

BREADS
BISCUITS
MUFFINS

BLUEBERRY MUFFINS

2 cups blueberries, *washed, stems removed*

3 cups flour

1¼ cups sugar

4½ teaspoons baking powder

½ teaspoon baking soda

½ teaspoon salt

1¼ cups milk

1 cup (2 sticks) butter, *melted*

2 eggs, *lightly beaten*

Preheat the oven to 400° F. Line muffin tin with paper liners. Toss the blueberries with 2 tablespoons of the flour and set aside. Sift the remaining flour, sugar, baking powder, baking soda, and salt together into a large bowl. Add the milk, butter, and eggs and stir until just combined. Gently fold in the blueberries and spoon the batter into the prepared muffin tins. Bake for 20 to 25 minutes, until the tops are browned and a toothpick inserted in the center of one of the muffins comes out clean. Let the muffins cool in the tins on a wire rack, then remove the muffins from the tins.

Makes 18 regular muffins or 12 large ones.

MILE-HIGH BISCUITS

3 cups flour, plus more for rolling
out the dough

1 tablespoon sugar

2 tablespoons baking powder

1 teaspoon salt

½ cup butter

1 egg

½ cup milk

Preheat the oven to 450°F. Sift the flour, sugar, baking powder, and salt together into a large bowl. Using a pastry blender or your fingertips, cut in the butter until the mixture resembles coarse meal. In a small bowl, combine the egg and milk, then add it to the flour mixture all at once, stirring with a fork just enough to make a soft dough that holds together in a ball. Turn the dough out onto a lightly floured surface and knead lightly 15 times, about 30 seconds. Roll the dough out about ¾ inch inch thick. With a floured 2-inch biscuit cutter, cut out biscuits; place them 1 inch apart on an ungreased baking sheet. Gather up the scraps, handling the dough as little as possible, and roll out and cut more biscuits. Bake for 12 to 15 minutes, until golden brown. Serve immediately.

Makes 16 biscuits.

GRIDDLE CAKES

1 cup all-purpose flour

½ teaspoon salt

1 teaspoon sugar

2 teaspoons baking powder

1 egg, *separated*

2 tablespoons butter, *melted*

1 cup milk

butter and syrup, for serving

Sift the flour, sugar, baking powder, and salt together into a large bowl. Add the egg yolk, melted butter, and milk and beat until the batter is thoroughly combined. In a separate bowl, whisk the egg white until it holds stiff peaks, then gently fold it into the batter. Let the batter stand for 10 minutes; do not stir again. Place a large ungreased griddle over medium-high heat . When the griddle is hot, ladle about ¼-cupfuls of batter onto the griddle to make 4-inch cakes. Cook until browned on the bottom, about 2 minutes, then turn and cook until the other side is browned, about 1½ minutes. Serve immediately with butter and syrup.

Makes about 10 griddle cakes.

FRENCH TOAST

1 egg	pinch of salt
½ cup milk	2 tablespoons butter
1 teaspoon sugar	4 slices of bread

Break the egg into a shallow dish large enough to hold the bread. A pie plate is perfect for this. Add the milk, sugar, and salt and beat with a fork. In a large skillet over medium heat, melt 1 tablespoon of the butter. Dip one piece of bread into the egg mixture, coating each side thoroughly. Using a spatula, transfer the coated bread slices to the skillet. Cook until nicely browned on the bottom, about 5 minutes, then turn over and brown the other side. Cook the remaining pieces of bread the same way adding butter to the skillet as needed. Serve hot with maple syrup, cinnamon sugar, or jam.

Serves 2.

WAFFLES

1¾ cups flour

1 tablespoon baking powder

1 tablespoon sugar

½ teaspoon salt

3 eggs, *well beaten*

1½ cups milk

½ cup butter, *melted*

½ cup blueberries, or

raisins, or

chocolate chips, or

banana slices, or

bacon bits

Preheat a waffle iron. In a medium bowl, mix together the flour, baking powder, sugar, and salt. In a separate bowl, whisk together the eggs, milk, and butter. Pour the egg mixture into the dry ingredients and whisk until the batter is thoroughly combined. If desired, gently fold in the blueberries, raisins, chocolate chips, bananas, or bacon bits. Ladle about ½ cup of the batter onto the waffle iron, spread it to the edges of the iron with the back of a spoon, and close the lid. Cook until golden brown, about 2 minutes depending on your waffle iron. Serve immediately with butter and syrup.

Makes 6 round Belgian waffles, or 12 square waffles.

HOW TO COOK RICE & PASTA

HOW TO COOK RICE

1 cup long-grain white rice

1 teaspoon salt

Put 2 cups of water and the salt in a heavy saucepan and bring to a boil. Add the rice, stir, and bring back to a boil, then lower the heat so that the water is just simmering. Cover the saucepan and simmer for about 20 minutes, or until all the water is absorbed and the rice is tender. Gently fluff the rice with a fork and serve hot. Makes 3 cups rice.

HOW TO COOK PASTA

½ pound (8 ounces) pasta

1 teaspoon salt

Put 8 cups water and the salt in a large pot and bring to a boil. Add the pasta and stir to make sure the pasta isn't sticking to the bottom and that the pasta is covered with the water. Boil for 9 to 12 minutes, until done. To test for doneness, use a long-handled fork or pasta server to lift out a piece of pasta. Run it under cold water for a few seconds, then bite into it. If it is tender, and if the center is cooked through, the pasta is done. If it is still hard, let the pasta cook for 1 to 2 minutes longer.

Place a large colander in the sink. Very carefully carry the pasta pot to the sink and slowly pour the water and pasta into the colander and let the pasta drain. Shake the colander a few times to help remove the water. You can return the pasta to the pot and stir in the sauce or, serve the pasta in individual bowls with the sauce on top. In either case, serve while hot.

Serves 2.

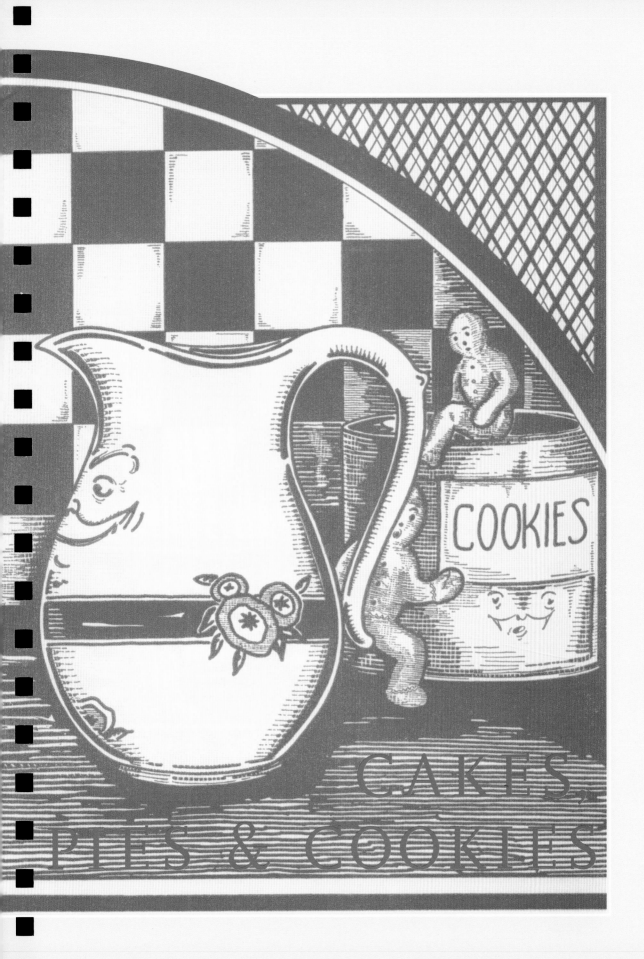

COOKIES

CAKES, PIES & COOKIES

BIRTHDAY CAKE

1½ cups all-purpose flour,
   plus more for the pans

2 teaspoons baking powder

¼ teaspoon salt

½ cup (1 stick) butter, *softened*,
   plus more for the pans

1 cup sugar

2 eggs, *beaten*

½ cup milk

1 teaspoon vanilla extract

frosting of your choice (see page 83)

Preheat oven to 350°F. Butter and flour two 8-inch cake pans. Sift the flour, baking powder, and salt together into a medium bowl and set aside.

Using an electric mixer, cream the butter and sugar together until light and fluffy, about 2 minutes. Add the eggs and beat well. Add half of the flour mixture, stir well, then add half of the milk and the vanilla. Add the remaining flour mixture, stir, then add the remaining milk and stir until the batter is smooth. Divide the batter between the prepared pans and bake for about 25 minutes, until the top of the cake is golden brown and springs back when you press the center lightly with your finger. Let the cakes cool in the pans for 10 minutes, then use a thin knife to loosen the sides of the cakes and turn them out onto wire racks to cool. Wait until the cakes are completely cool before frosting them, or the frosting will melt and run off the cake. Makes one 2-layer cake.

CHOCOLATE
BIRTHDAY CAKE

2 ounces (2 squares) unsweetened chocolate

1½ cups all-purpose flour

1 teaspoon baking soda

⅛ teaspoon salt

½ cup butter, plus more for the pans

1½ cups sugar

2 eggs

½ cup milk

1 teaspoon vanilla extract

½ cup boiling water

frosting of your choice (see page 83)

Preheat the oven to 350° F. Prepare 2, 8-inch cake pans. Line the bottoms of the pans with waxed paper or parchment paper cut into circles to fit, then butter the paper. In a small saucepan over very low heat, melt the chocolate, then set it aside to cool. Sift the flour, baking soda, and salt together into a medium bowl and set aside.

Using an electric mixer, cream the butter and sugar together until light and fluffy, about 2 minutes. Add the eggs, one at a time, beating well after each addition. Beat in the cooled chocolate, milk, and vanilla. Gradually add the flour mixture and stir well, then add the boiling water and mix until the batter is smooth. Divide the batter between the prepared pans and bake for about 30 minutes, until a toothpick inserted in the center comes out clean. Let the cakes cool in the pans for 10 minutes, then use a thin knife to loosen the sides of the cakes and turn them out onto wire racks to cool. Peel off the paper. Wait until the cakes are completely cool before frosting them, or the frosting will melt and run off the cake.

Makes one 2-layer cake.

Boy! What Frosting

CHOCOLATE FROSTING

6 ounces (6 squares) unsweetened
  chocolate

½ cup unsalted butter

4 cups confectioners' sugar

2 eggs

2 teaspoons vanilla extract

In a small heavy saucepan over very low heat, melt the chocolate and butter together. Remove from the heat and add 4 tablespoons water. Stir to blend well and let the mixture cool slightly. Transfer to a medium bowl and, using an electric mixer, beat in half of the confectioner's sugar a little at a time. Add the eggs and beat well, then add the remaining confectioner's sugar and the vanilla and beat until the frosting reaches spreading consistency, about 4 minutes.

Makes enough to frost one 8-inch 2-layer cake.

WHITE HONEY FROSTING

1 egg white

½ cup honey

pinch of salt

This frosting has a strong honey flavor. If you prefer a plain vanilla flavor, use white corn syrup in place of the honey and add ½ teaspoon vanilla.

In a large bowl, combine all the ingredients. Using an electric mixer, beat on high speed for 10 to 12 minutes, until the frosting is glossy and white and forms stiff peaks when the beaters are lifted.

Makes enough to frost one 8-inch 2-layer cake.

STRAWBERRY SHORTCAKE

1 recipe MILE-HIGH
BISCUITS (see page 68) or
1 recipe BIRTHDAY CAKE
(see page 79)

3 pints strawberries
½ cup sugar
1 tablespoon lemon juice
whipped cream

Wash the strawberries and remove the hulls (the green leaves). Put aside several of the nicest-looking berries to decorate the top. Slice the remaining berries in half, or, if they are very big, into several slices. Put the sliced berries in a bowl and add the sugar and lemon juice; stir very gently to combine. Set aside at room temperature for about 1 hour to let the sugar dissolve and for the berries to release some of their juices.

TO MAKE THE SHORTCAKE WITH BISCUITS: *Using a fork, gently split the biscuits in half horizontally and place the bottom halves on serving plates. Spoon the strawberry mixture over the biscuit bottom and set the other half on top. Garnish with whipped cream and and one of the whole strawberries. Serve immediately. This is especially delicious if you serve it while the biscuits are still warm from the oven.*

TO MAKE THE SHORTCAKE WITH LAYER CAKE: *Place one cake layer on a serving plate (upside down) and spoon half of the strawberry mixture over the cake. Set the second cake layer on top (again, upside down) and spoon the remaining berry mixture over the top. Cover the top with whipped cream and decorate with the whole strawberries. Slice and serve immediately. Serves 6 to 8.*

BROWNIES

½ cup (1 stick) butter,
    plus more for the pan

4 ounces (4 squares) unsweetened
    chocolate

2 cups sugar

3 eggs, *lightly beaten*

2 teaspoons vanilla extract

1 cup all-purpose flour

½ teaspoon salt

1 cup walnuts, *chopped* (optional)

Preheat the oven to 350°F. Line a 9-by-13-inch baking pan with aluminum foil and butter the foil. In a heavy saucepan over low heat, melt the butter and chocolate together. Pour the mixture into a large bowl and let it cool. Stir in the sugar and mix well. Stir in the eggs and vanilla, then stir in the flour, salt, and walnuts, if desired. Pour the batter into the prepared pan, spread evenly, and bake for 25 to 30 minutes, or until a toothpick inserted in the center comes out clean. Let the pan cool completely, then lift the brownies out using the foil. Cut into 12 squares.

Makes 1 dozen brownies.

SUGAR COOKIES

4 cups all-purpose flour

2½ teaspoons baking powder

¾ teaspoon salt

1 cup (2 sticks) butter

1 cup sugar, plus more for
   shaping the cookies

2 eggs

3 teaspoons vanilla extract

Preheat oven to 400°F. Sift the flour, baking powder, and salt together in a medium bowl and set aside.

Using an electric mixer, cream the butter and sugar together until light and fluffy. Add the eggs, one at a time, then beat in the vanilla. Gradually mix in the flour mixture. Pinch off bits of dough and roll them into 1-inch balls. Place them about 2-inches apart on an ungreased cookie sheet. Butter the bottom of a wide, flat-bottomed drinking glass. Dip the bottom in sugar, and press down on each ball of dough until it is about an 1/8-inch thick circle. You won't have to butter the bottom of the glass each time, but you do need to dip the bottom in the sugar each time. Bake for 10 to 12 minutes, until edges are lightly browned. Remove the cookies to a wire rack to cool and repeat with the remaining dough.

Makes about 4½ dozen cookies.

The chocolate chip cookie was invented by Ruth Graves Wakefield over seventy years ago. In 1930 she and her husband, Kenneth, bought an old toll house just outside of Whitman, Massachusetts. They opened a restaurant and lodge in the toll house, and visitors would travel from miles around to sample Mrs. Wakefield's baked goods. When she was preparing the batter for a batch of her Butter Drop Do cookies she realized she didn't have any baker's chocolate, so she cut up a Nestlé's semi-sweet chocolate bar and added it to the dough. Her creation was an instant favorite. In exchange for a lifetime supply of chocolate chips, Mrs. Wakefield gave Nestlé permission to print the recipe on the package, which they have been doing ever since.

NESTLÉ TOLL HOUSE COOKIES

2¼ cups all-purpose flour

1 teaspoon baking soda

1 teaspoon salt

1 cup (2 sticks) butter, *softened*

¾ cup granulated sugar

¾ cup brown sugar, *packed*

1 teaspoon vanilla extract

2 eggs

2 cups (12-ounce package) semisweet chocolate chips

1 cup chopped nuts (optional)

Preheat oven to 375°F. Combine flour, baking soda, and salt in a small bowl. Beat butter, granulated sugar, brown sugar, and vanilla extract in a large bowl until creamy. Add eggs, one at a time, beating well after each addition. Gradually beat in flour mixture. Stir in morsels and nuts. Drop by rounded tablespoon onto ungreased baking sheets. Bake for 9 to 12 minutes or until golden brown. Let stand for 2 minutes: remove to wire racks to cool completely.

Makes about 5 dozen cookies.

This recipe has been adapted from the book Ruth Wakefield's Tried and True Toll House Recipes.

PEANUT BUTTER COOKIES

1½ cups all-purpose flour

½ teaspoon baking soda

1/8 teaspoon salt

½ cup (1 stick) butter, *softened,*
   plus more for the cookie sheets

½ cup peanut butter

½ cup sugar

½ cup brown sugar

1 large egg

½ teaspoon vanilla extract

Sift the flour, baking soda, and salt together into a medium bowl and set aside. Using an electric mixer, cream the butter, peanut butter, and the sugars together until light in color, about 2 minutes. Add the egg and vanilla and mix well. Gradually add the flour mixture and mix until it is thoroughly incorporated. Cover the dough with plastic wrap and chill it in the refrigerator for at least 1 hour or as long as overnight. Preheat the oven to 350°F. Pinch off bits of dough and roll them into 1-inch balls. Place the balls 2 inches apart on a greased cookie sheet, then flatten the balls with a fork in a criss-cross pattern. Bake for about 14 minutes, until lightly browned around the edges. Remove the cookies to a wire rack to cool and repeat with the remaining dough.

Makes 32 cookies.

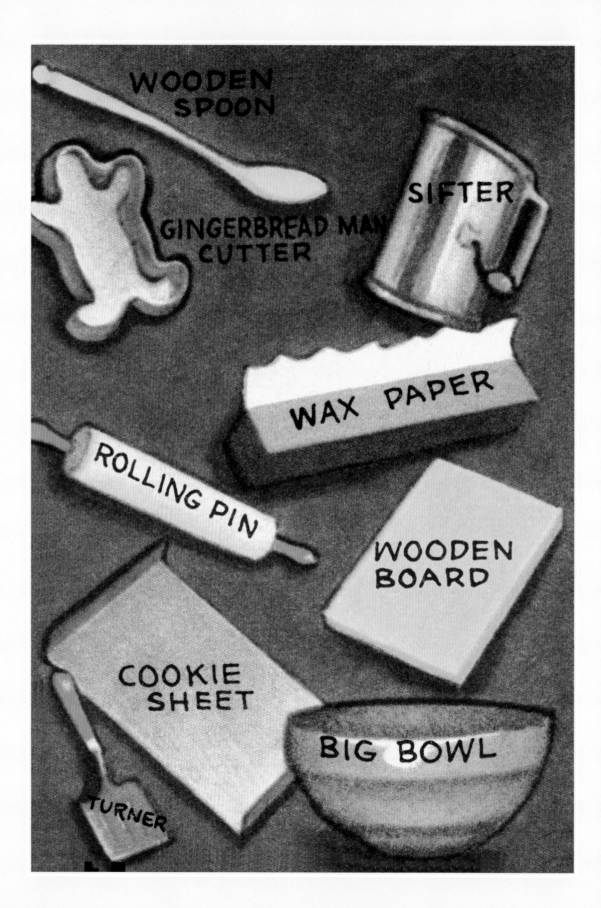

GINGERBREAD MEN

3 cups all-purpose flour

2 teaspoons baking powder

½ teaspoon baking soda

½ teaspoon salt

2 teaspoons ground ginger

½ cup brown sugar

½ cup butter, at room temperature,
    plus more for the cookie sheets

1 egg, *beaten*

½ cup molasses

Dried currants or raisins,
    for decorating

Sift the flour, baking powder, baking soda, salt, and ginger together into a medium bowl and set aside. Using an electric mixer, cream the butter and brown sugar together until light and fluffy, about 2 minutes. Add the egg and molasses and beat well. Gradually add the flour mixture and stir until the dough is thoroughly combined and comes together in a ball. Divide the dough in half and wrap each ball in plastic wrap; chill in the refrigerator for several hours or overnight.

Preheat the oven to 350°F. Using a floured rolling pin, roll out one ball of the dough at a time on a lightly floured surface to ¼ inch thick. Lightly flour a cookie cutter and cut out gingerbread men; use a spatula to carefully transfer them to the prepared cookie sheets, 1 inch apart. Press currants or raisins into the cookies to make eyes, mouth, and buttons. Gather up the scraps and roll out and cut more cookies. Bake for 10 minutes. Let the cookies cool on the pan for 5 minutes, then remove them to wire racks to cool. Repeat with the remaining dough.

Makes about 2 dozen 5-inch-tall gingerbread men.

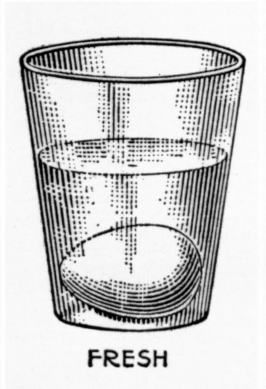

FRESH

3 WEEKS

3 MONTHS

OLDER

FORGOTTEN COOKIES
CHOCOLATE CHIP AND NUT MERINGUES

4 egg whites, at room temperature

¼ teaspoon salt

1 teaspoon vanilla extract

¾ cup sugar

1 cup almonds, *sliced* or
  pecans, *chopped*

1 cup mini semisweet chocolate chips

Preheat the oven to 225°F. Line two cookie sheets with parchment paper. Using an electric mixer, beat the egg whites at medium speed until foamy and white, about 2 minutes. Add the salt and beat at high speed for 1 minute, until just stiff. Reduce the speed to medium and add the vanilla. Continue to beat, adding the sugar a few tablespoons at a time, until the mixture is smooth and glossy, about 3 minutes longer. Very gently fold in the nuts and chocolate chips. Using a tablespoon drop the meringue in dolops 1 inch apart from each other on the cookie sheets (the meringues will not spread). Bake for 45 minutes, then turn off the oven, and let the meringues sit in a closed oven overnight.

Remove from the oven the next morning and store in an airtight container.
Makes about 40 meringues.

It's important to use fresh eggs when cooking. You can tell if an egg is fresh by placing it in a glass of water. A fresh egg will lie at the bottom of the glass.

THE WONDERFUL COOKIE

OATMEAL CRISPS

¾ cup all-purpose flour

½ teaspoon baking soda

¼ teaspoon salt

¼ teaspoon each of ground
   cinnamon, ginger, and nutmeg

½ cup (1 stick) butter, at room
   temperature, plus more for
   the cookie sheets

½ cup sugar

½ cup light brown sugar

1 egg

½ teaspoon vanilla extract

1½ cups rolled oats (not instant)

½ cup raisins *or* dried cranberries

½ cup walnuts, *chopped,* or
   ½ cup chocolate chips

Preheat oven to 350°F and lightly butter two cookie sheets. Sift the flour, baking soda, salt, cinnamon, nutmeg, and ginger together into a medium bowl and set aside.

Using an electric mixer, cream the butter together with the ½ cup granulated sugar and ½ cup light brown sugar until light and fluffy, about 2 minutes. Beat in the egg and vanilla. Stir in the oats, then gradually add the flour mixture and stir until thoroughly combined. Stir in the raisins and nuts. Drop rounded-teaspoon-size balls of dough 2½-inches apart on the cookie sheets. Bake for 12 to 15 minutes, until lightly browned around the edges. Let the cookies cool on the cookie sheets for 1 minute, then use a thin spatula to remove them to wire racks to cool. Repeat with the remaining dough.

Makes 5 dozen cookies.

PIE CRUST

2 cups all-purpose flour,
plus more for rolling out

10 tablespoons chilled unsalted

butter, *cut into pieces*

½ teaspoon salt

10 tablespoons ice water, or more

Sift the flour and salt together into a medium bowl. Using a pastry blender or your fingertips, cut the butter into the flour mixture until it resembles coarse meal. Sprinkle 10 tablespoons ice water over the mixture and use a fork or the pastry blender to toss the mixture together, adding more water, a little at a time, until you can gather the dough into a ball with your hands. Handling the dough as little as possible, form it into two balls and wrap them in plastic wrap. Refrigerate the dough for at least 1 hour or up to 2 days. You can even freeze the dough for up to 1 month; thaw it in the refrigerator for 1 day before using it. Makes enough dough for two 9-inch single-crust pies, or one 9-inch double-crust pie.

TO ROLL OUT THE DOUGH : *Work with one ball of dough at a time. Sprinkle the work surface with a little flour. Unwrap the dough and place it on the flour. Starting in the center and using even pressure, roll the rolling pin away from you toward the outer edge. Give the dough a ¼ turn, sprinkle with more flour and roll out from the center again. Repeat the rolling, turning and flouring until*

you have a circle about 1/8-inch thick. Hold the pie plate over the dough to make sure the circle is about 2 inches wider than the plate all around.

TO LIFT PIE CRUST : *Wrap the dough over the rolling pin and lift it over the pie plate. Unroll the dough evenly onto the plate. Gently press the dough into the bottom. If making a single-crust pie, trim the excess, roll the edge under, then crimp as in the picture above. If making a double-crust pie, spoon the filling into the bottom crust, roll out the second ball of dough and cover the filling. Press the edges together to seal the two crusts. Trim away the excess, leaving 1 inch hanging over the edge. Roll the edge under then pinch the edge to crimp, as above. With the tip of a knife, cut 2 or 3 slits in the top crust so the steam can escape while baking.*

APPLE PIE

4 cups (4 to 5 medium) apples
   peeled, cored, and sliced

2 teaspoons fresh lemon juice

¼ cup all-purpose flour

½ cup sugar

½ teaspoon ground cinnamon

3 tablespoons butter, *cut into pieces*

1 recipe PIE CRUST (see page 98)

1 egg yolk, *lightly beaten and mixed*
   with 1 teaspoon water

Preheat oven to 425°F. In a large bowl, combine the apples, lemon juice, flour, sugar, and cinnamon; set aside.

Roll out two pie crusts according to the directions on page 99. Place the bottom crust on a 9-inch pie plate, gently pressing the dough into the bottom of the pan. Pour the apple mixture into the bottom crust and dot with the butter. Cover the apples with the top crust, crimping the top and bottom crusts together all around and trimming off the excess dough. With a small knife, cut vents in the top crust to allow steam to escape while the pie bakes.

Brush the top crust and the crimped edge with the egg yolk mixture. This will help the top crust brown nicely. Bake for about 45 minutes, until the top is golden brown all over. Let the pie cool on a wire rack for at least 30 minutes before slicing. Serves 6 to 8.

PUMPKIN
Jack O'Lantern

FERRY-MORSE SEEDS

39¢

NET WT 4.16 G

EXCELLENT for FREEZING

PUMPKIN PIE

½ recipe PIE CRUST dough
  (see page 98)
1¼ cups (most of a 15-ounce can)
  pumpkin purée
¾ cup sugar
½ teaspoon salt
¼ teaspoon gound ginger

1 teaspoon ground cinnamon
1 teaspoon all-purpose flour
2 eggs, *lightly beaten*
1 cup evaporated milk
2 tablespoons water
½ teaspoon vanilla extract

Preheat the oven to 400°F. Roll out one pie crust according to the directions on page 99. Place the crust on a 9-inch pie plate, gently pressing the dough into the bottom of the plate. Trim and crimp the edge and set aside.

In a large bowl, combine the pumpkin, sugar, salt, ginger, cinnamon, and flour. Add the eggs and mix well. Stir in the evaporated milk, water, and vanilla. Pour the mixture into the pie crust and bake for 45 to 50 minutes, until a knife inserted in the center of the pie comes out clean. Serve at room temperature.

Serves 8.

MORE
DESSERTS

CHOCOLATE PUDDING

5 tablespoons sugar

2 tablespoons unsweetened cocoa
   powder

2 tablespoons cornstarch

1/8 teaspoon salt

2½ cups milk

2 eggs

1¼ cups (8 ounces) semisweet
   chocolate chips

1 teaspoon vanilla extract

whipped cream (optional)

In a heavy saucepan, whisk together the sugar, cocoa powder, cornstarch, and salt. Add the milk and eggs and whisk until there are no lumps. Stir in the chocolate chips. Place over medium heat and cook, stirring constantly, until the mixture comes to a full boil. Remove from the heat and stir in the vanilla. Pour the pudding into a large serving bowl or individual dishes. Top with whipped cream if desired. You can serve the pudding warm, room temperature or chilled. If you aren't going to serve the pudding right away, cover with plastic wrap placed directly on the surface (to prevent a skin from forming). Cool to room temperature, then chill in the refrigerator and serve cold, with whipped cream if desired.

Serves 6.

MAMIE EISENHOWER'S MILLION DOLLAR FUDGE

2 cups sugar

pinch of salt

1 tablespoon butter,

  plus more for the pan

1 cup evaporated milk

12 ounces semisweet chocolate,

  chips or squares

1 cup marshmallow fluff

½ teaspoon vanilla extract

Lightly butter a 9-by-12-inch baking dish or pan. In a heavy 2-quart saucepan, combine the sugar, salt, butter, and evaporated milk and bring to a boil. Boil the syrup for 7 minutes, watching the pan closely because the syrup can boil over easily.

Meanwhile, put the chocolate chips, marshmallow fluff, and vanilla in a large heat-proof bowl. Very carefully pour the boiling syrup over the chocolate mixture and stir well, until the chocolate is melted and the mixture is smooth. Pour into the prepared pan. Let cool to room temperature, then chill in the refrigerator until firm. Cut into squares, remove them from the pan with a metal spatula, and serve.

Makes about 80 small pieces of fudge.

BAKED APPLES

4 large baking apples

¼ cup brown sugar

1 teaspoon ground cinammon

¼ cup raisins

1 teaspoon lemon rind, *grated*

2 tablespoons butter

vanilla ice cream (optional)

Preheat oven to 350°F. Wash the apples. With a melon baller, remove the core of the apples, stopping within ½ inch at the bottom of the cavity. With a vegetable peeler, remove the skin from around the top third of the apple so it looks like it has a white cap. Put the apples into a baking dish big enough to hold them without crowding. Combine the sugar, raisins and spices and spoon the mixture into the apple. Top each with a tablespoon of butter. Pour 2/3 cup water into the bottom of the pan. Cover with a lid or foil. Bake for 30 minutes until the apples are soft but not mushy. Uncover the apples, spoon some of the liquid over the top and bake for 10 more minutes. Serve while warm or at room temperature, with vanilla ice cream if desired.

Serves 4.

ANY KIND OF FRUIT SALAD

ANY COMBINATION OF FRUIT:

Apples	Blueberries	½ cup water
Pears	Oranges	½ cup honey
Peaches	Grapefruit	2 or 3 slices
Plums	Raspberries	fresh ginger
Grapes	Blackberries	2 or 3 slices
Cantaloupe	Bananas	fresh lemon
Strawberries		(optional)

TO PREPARE THE FRUIT: *Slice, peel, core or pit the larger fruits, and slice and remove the rind from cantaloupes, oranges, or grapefruits. Place the prepared fruit in a large bowl; if you're using raspberries, blackberries, strawberries, bananas or other soft fruit, set them aside and add them to the salad just before serving to keep them from getting mushy. You should have at least 4 cups of fruit, but there is enough syrup for more. Think about which fruits look good together as well as what tastes good together. Try and use fruits that are in season, they will look and taste better.*

In a medium-size heavy saucepan, combine the water, honey, ginger, and lemon, if using, and bring to a boil. Simmer for 5 minutes, or until slightly thickened; watch the pan carefully to make sure the syrup doesn't boil over. Pour the hot syrup over the fruit and gently mix to combine. Let the salad cool to room temperature. Remove ginger and lemon slices before serving.

Serves 4 to 6.

SNACKS

DEVILED EGGS

4 large eggs

2 tablespoons mayonnaise

½ teaspoon prepared mustard

¼ teaspoon salt

2 teaspoons chopped parsley,
  chives, or dill

When cool enough to handle, tap the eggs lightly on a hard surface to crack the shells all over, then remove the shells. Make sure you get every piece of shell off of the eggs. Cut the eggs in half lengthwise. Carefully remove the yolks from the whites and place them in a small bowl; set the whites aside.

With a fork, mash the yolks together with the mayonnaise, mustard, and salt. Stir in the parsley (or sprinkle the parsley on top after you fill the whites). Using a small spoon, scoop the yolk mixture into the whites.

Serve at room temperature. You can serve them balanced on a lettuce leaf as pictured. Makes 8 deviled eggs.

HOW TO BOIL AN EGG

Put the eggs in a saucepan and cover with cold water by 1 inch. Place the saucepan over medium-high heat and bring to a boil; lower the heat and simmer for 12 minutes. Remove the saucepan from the heat. Use a large spoon to get each egg out of the water; transfer to a bowl. Then run cold water over the eggs to stop the cooking process and to cool the eggs so you will be able to peel them.

EQUIPMENT NEEDED

MEASURING SPOONS

SPATULA

SHALLOW PAN

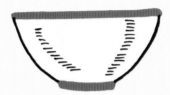

BOWL

BUTTER KNIFE

INGREDIENTS

1 TEASPOON CINNAMON

4 TEASPOONS SUGAR

2 SLICES BREAD

2 TABLESPOONS BUTTER

CINNAMON TOAST

4 teaspoons sugar

1 teaspoon ground cinnamon

2 slices of bread

2 tablespoons butter, *softened*

Preheat the oven or toaster oven to broil. Mix the cinnamon and sugar together and set aside. Butter the bread. Sprinkle the cinnamon sugar evenly over the bread. Place the bread in a shallow pan or on a cookie sheet. Place the pan under the broiler and watch through the window of the oven until bread is toasted and butter and the cinnamon sugar has melted. Remove with a spatula since the toast is now very hot.

EGG IN A HOLE

Break an egg into a cup.

Cut a hole in the middle of a slice of bread
with a cookie cutter or a small glass.

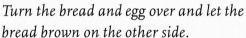

The bread should look like this.

Melt a tablespoon of butter in a frying pan
over medium heat.

Place the bread in the pan.

Drop the egg into the hole. It may not all fit in the hole,
but that's okay. Cook until the egg is "set"
and the bread is lightly browned on the bottom.

Turn the bread and egg over and let the
bread brown on the other side.

Serve hot.

GRILLED CHEESE SANDWICH

1 or 2 slices of cheese

  (about 2 ounces)

2 slices of bread

2 tablespoons butter

Place the cheese on one slice of the bread, then cover with the other slice and set aside. At this point you can also add sliced tomato, cooked bacon, and/or mustard, if you would like. In a skillet or on a griddle over medium heat, melt 1 tablespoon of the butter. Slide the sandwich into the skillet and cook until the bottom is nicely browned. Use a spatula to turn the sandwich over and cook until the other side is browned and the cheese has melted. Add the remaining butter to the skillet if necessary. Remove from the pan with a spatula and serve while hot.

Serves 1.

POPCORN BALLS

5 quarts popped popcorn

salt to taste

1 cup salted peanuts or

    dried cranberries, or

    ½ cup of each (optional)

2 cups sugar

1 cup light corn syrup

1 tablespoon molasses

½ cup (1 stick) butter

1 teaspoon vanilla extract

If you use a candy thermometer when you make these, they are very easy. Otherwise, you have to guess about the temperature, and the temperature of the syrup is very important.

Remove and discard any unpopped kernels and place the popcorn, salt, and peanuts and cranberries if you are using them, in a very large bowl; set aside.

In a heavy saucepan over medium heat, combine the sugar, corn syrup, molasses, butter, and 1/4 cup water. Bring to a boil, watching the pan closely, then lower the heat and simmer until the syrup just reaches the hard ball stage (260°F on a candy thermometer). This may take up to 15 minutes. As soon as the syrup reaches the right temperature, remove from the heat and stir in the vanilla. Working quickly but very carefully pour the syrup evenly over the popcorn and toss with two big spoons as if you're tossing a salad. As soon as the popcorn is cool enough to handle, but while it's still warm, gather and press the popcorn into balls the size of baseballs. Butter your hands to prevent sticking. Let cool completely, then wrap in waxed paper. Makes about 1 dozen popcorn balls.

BEVERAGES

HOT COCOA

2 large marshmallows (optional)

¼ cup sugar

¼ cup unsweetened cocoa powder

pinch of salt

½ cup warm water

2 cups milk

1/8 teaspoon vanilla extract

Put a marshmallow in the bottom of each of 2 mugs and set aside. In a heavy saucepan, whisk together the sugar, cocoa powder, and salt until there are no lumps. Add the water and bring to a boil over medium heat. Lower the heat and simmer for 3 minutes. Add the milk, whisk to combine, and bring almost to a boil over medium heat. Remove from the heat and stir in the vanilla. Ladle the cocoa into the mugs and serve very hot.

Serves 2.

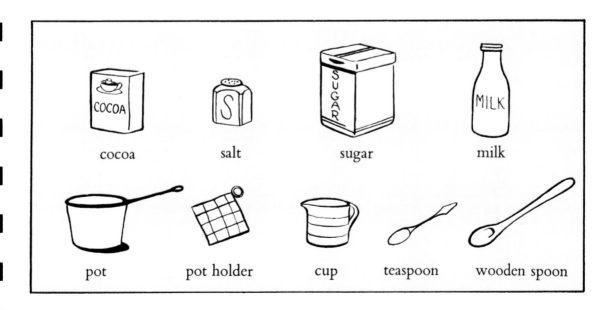

cocoa   salt   sugar   milk

pot   pot holder   cup   teaspoon   wooden spoon

IT'S SO IMPORTANT TO DRINK WATER !

Did you know that more than half of your body weight is from water? Water keeps our bodies running smoothly by delivering nutrients and carrying away the waste. It also lubricates your joints making it possible to move. It is especially important to drink water before and after you exercise because it helps to regulate your body temperature. When you sweat, water evaporates through the skin to help the body stay cool. Did you know that food, especially fruits and vegetables, also contains a lot of water? One apple contains four ounces of water and a banana has almost three ounces. But water from food is not enough to keep your body hydrated. You need to drink at least eight glasses of water every day.

70%
WATER

LEMONADE

UTENSILS:

Spoon   Measuring cup   Water   Orange Squeezer   Saucepan

INGREDIENTS:

Cold water   1/2 cup water   1/2 cup lemon juice

Ice cubes   1/2 cup sugar

PROCEDURE:

1.

Boil sugar   and water   together in saucepan

for 5 minutes to make syrup.

2. Cool. Add lemon juice

---

3. Place in pitcher and

add quart of cold water

6 ice cubes

Stir with spoon

CHOCOLATE
ICE CREAM SODA

1 scoop vanilla ice cream

club soda or seltzer water

2 tablespoons chocolate syrup

whipped cream

cherry or strawberry

Fill a glass half full with soda. Add the chocolate syrup and stir well. Add a scoop of ice cream and fill the glass almost to the top with more soda or seltzer. Stir again.

Top with whipped cream and a cherry or strawberry if desired.

It is customary to drink this with a straw.

Serves 1.

MILKSHAKE

1 cup milk

2 scoops (about 4 ounces) vanilla ice cream

ADD ONE OF THE FOLLOWING

IF DESIRED:

¼ cup chocolate syrup

or

1 banana, *sliced*

or

6 strawberries, *sliced*

or

6 chocolate wafer cookies, *crumbled*

Put all the ingredients in the jar of a blender. Have an adult help

you use the blender. Blend until smooth. Pour into 2 glasses.

Serves 2.

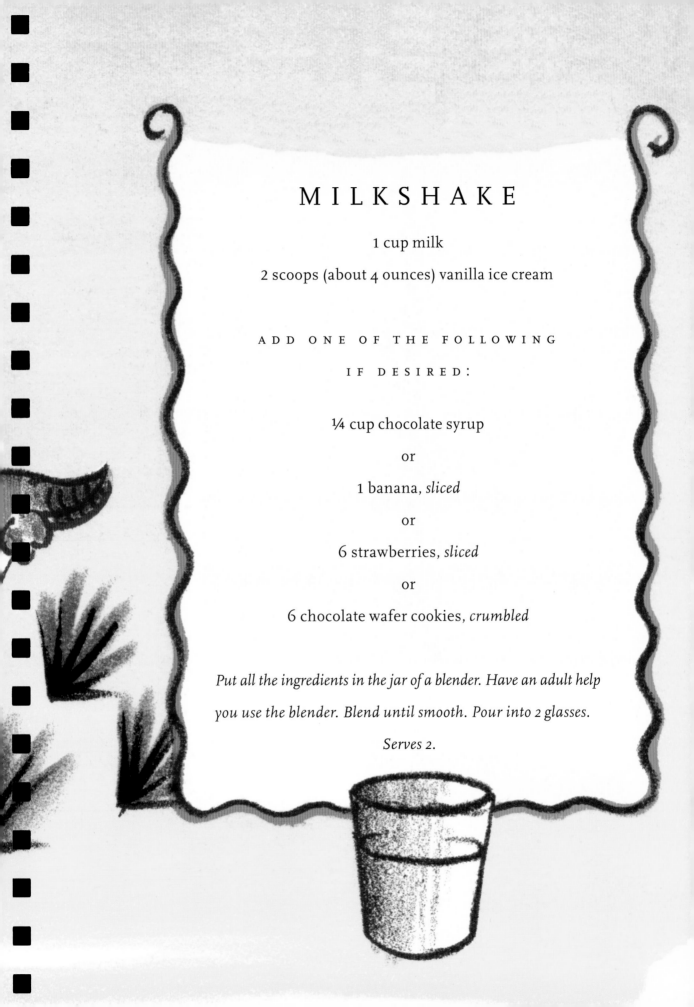

THE
TABLETOP

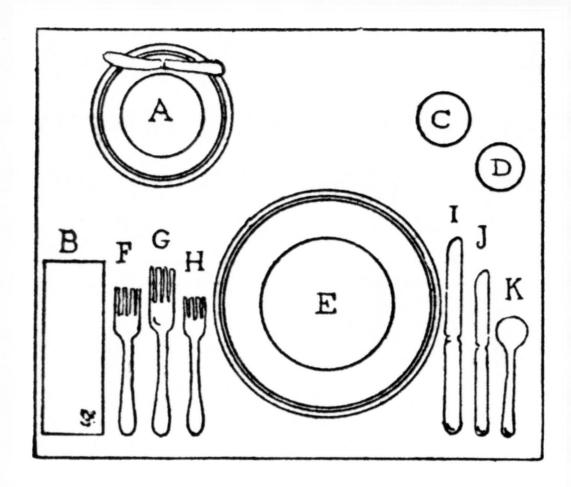

A. *Bread and butter plate, butter knife*

B. *Napkin (fold lengthwise)*

C. *Water goblet or glass*

D. *Smaller goblet*

E. *Place or service plate*

F, G, H. *Entrée, main course, and salad forks*

I, J. *Main course and entrée knives*

K. *Soup spoon*

HOW TO SET YOUR TABLE

PUT YOUR MILK OR
WATER GLASS HERE

PUT YOUR NAPKIN
HERE — FOLDED

SALAD

SOUP

TEA

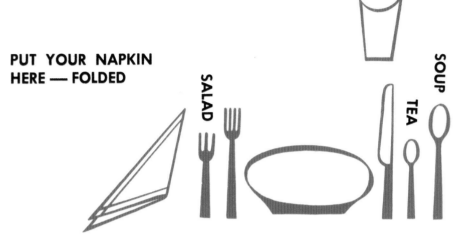

HERE'S WHERE YOUR
SILVERWARE GOES

AND HERE'S HOW YOUR
TABLE SHOULD LOOK
ALL READY TO SIT DOWN

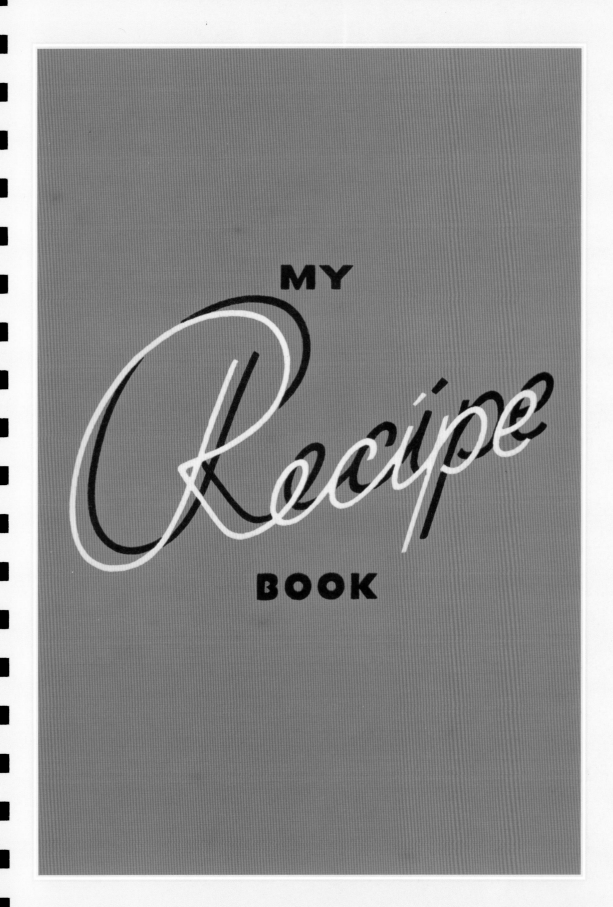

MY *Recipe* BOOK

My Favorite Recipes

My Favorite Recipes

My Favorite Recipes

My Favorite Recipes

My Favorite Recipes

My Favorite Recipes

My Favorite Recipes

My Favorite Recipes

My Favorite Recipes

My Favorite Recipes

My Favorite Recipes

My Favorite Recipes

My Favorite Recipes

My Favorite Recipes

My Favorite Recipes

My Favorite Recipes

egg beater

wooden bowl

measuring spoons

bread board

double boiler

measuring cup

custard cups

cookie sheet

PICTURE CREDITS

Cover *The Jolly Times Cookbook* by Marjorie Noble Osborn, Illustrations by Clarence Biers ©1934 Rand McNally Company, Chicago **Endpaper** *The Secret of Cookies Candies and Cakes* by Helen Jill Fletcher, Illustrations by Margaret Zimmerman ©1957 Z.E. Harvey Inc., Harvey House Publishers, Irvington-on-Hudson, New York. **Page 1** *Come and See The Pantry Family Story* by Isabel Poudfit, Illustrations by Caroline Whitehead ©1942 David McKay Company Publishers, Washington Square, Philadelphia. **Page 2** *Child Life Cookbook* by Clara Ingram Judson ©1926 RandMcNally & Company, New York. **Page 4** *Carnation Cook Book* by Mary Blake ©1938 The Carnation Company, Reprinted by permission of Nestlé. **Page 5** *Patty Pans: A Cook Book for Beginners* by Florence LaGanke, Illustrations by W. Prentice Phillips ©1929 LittleBrown & Co., Boston. **Page 5** *Meals for Small Families* by Jean Mowat ©1929 Laidlaw Brothers, Chicago. **Page 6** *Mary Alden's Cook Book for Children,* An R. H. Loeb Recipix Book, Pictures by Dorothy King ©1955 Wonder Books, Inc. **Page 7** *Children's Picture Cook Book* by Margaret Gossett, Designed by Elizabeth Dauber ©1944 Planned Books for Young People, William R. Scott, Inc. New York. **Pages 8–9** Publisher Unknown. **Page 10** *Kitchen Fun* by Louise Bell Price ©1933 The Harter Publishing Company, Cleveland, Ohio. **Page 12** *Cooking Made Easy,* Union Carbide and Carbon Chemicals Corporation. **Page 14** *A Cookbook for Girls and Boys* by Irma S. Rombauer ©1946 The Bobbs-Merrill Company, Indianapolis, NY. **Page 15** *Junior Jewish Cook Book* by Aunt Fanny ©1956 Ktav Publishing House Drawings by Cyla London. **Pages 16–17** *A Child's First Cook Book* by Alma S. Lach, Illustrations by Doris Stolberg ©Howt, New York. **Page 18** *Carnation Cook Book* by Mary Blake ©1938 The Carnation Company, Reprinted by permission of Nestlé. **Page 19** Publisher unknown. **Page 20** *Household Arts for Home and School,* Vol. II by Anna M. Cooley and Wilhelmina H. Spohr ©1920 The Macmillan Company, New York. **Pages 22–23** *Child Life Cookbook* by Clara Ingram Judson ©1926 Rand McNally, New York. **Page 24** *Things to Cook* by Helen Jill Fletcher ©1951 Paxton-Slade, New York. **Page 25** *A Recipe Primer* by Henrietta Fleck ©1949 D. C. Heath, Boston **Page 26** *Fun To Cook Book* © 1955 The Carnation Company, Reprinted by permission of Nestlé. **Pages 28–29** *Mary Alden's Cook Book* for Children An R. H. Loeb Recipix Book, Pictures by Dorothy King ©1955 Wonder Books. **Page 30** *The School Lunch* ©1928 Postum Company, Battle Creek, Michigan. **Pages 32–33** *Let's Cook Dinner* ©1946 Children's Press, Chicago, Scholastic Library Publishing. **Pages 34–35** *Household Arts for Home and School,* Vol. II by Anna M. Cooley and Wilhelmina H. Spohr ©1920 The Macmillan Company, New York. **Page 36** *Dishes Children Love* by Culinary Arts Institute, Illustrations by Beatrice Derwinski ©1954, 1955 Book Production Industries Inc. **Pages 38–39** *Jack and Jill: The Magazine for Boys and Girls* ©1939 The Curtis Publishing Company. **Page 40** *Mary Alden's Cook Book for Children,* An R. H. Loeb Recipix Book, Pictures by Dorothy King ©1955 Wonder Books. **Page 42** *Dishes Children Love* by Culinary Arts Institute, Illustrations by Beatrice Derwinski ©1954, 1955 Book Production Industries Inc. **Page 45** *Miss B.'s First Cookbook* by Peggy Hoffman ©1950 The Bobbs-Merrill Company, Inc. **Page 46** *This is the Book* by Janet Smalley, Published by Basil Blackwell, Oxford UK 1928. **Page 50** *Wolf in Chef's Clothing* by Robert H. Loeb, Jr. Illustrated by Jim Newhall ©1950 Wilcox & Follett Co., Chicago. **Page 51** *Dishes Children Love* by Culinary Arts Institute, Illustrations by Beatrice Derwinski © 1954, 1955 Book Production Industries Inc., **Pages 52–53** Publisher Unknown. **Pages 54–55** *Casserole Cooking Fun* by Barbara Guthrie McDonald, Illustrated by Vee Guthrie ©1967 Barbara Guthrie McDonald and Vee Guthrie, Published by Henry Z. Walck. **Pages 56–57** *Sunset's New Kitchen Cabinet,* ©1938, Sunset Publishing Corporation, Menlo Park. **Pages 58–59** *Maule's Seed Catalogue 1903,* William Henry

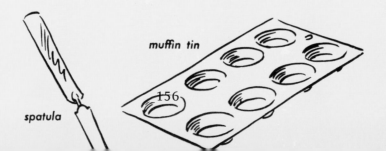
mixing bowls

spatula

muffin tin

cookie cutter

flour sifter

chopper

cake rack

wire whisk

Maule, Philadelphia. **Pages 60–61** *A Child's First Cook Book* by Alma S. Lach, Illustrations by Doris Stolberg. **Page 62** *Kitchen Magic* by Constance Cassady, Illustrations by James Reid© 1932 Florence Cassady. **Pages 64–65** *The Story Book of Foods from the Field* by Maud and Miska Petersham ©1936 John C. Winston Co. **Pages 66–67** *Child Life Cookbook* by Clara Ingram Judson ©1926 RandMcNally, New York. **Page 68** *Ryzon Baking Book* © 1917 General Chemical Company, New York. **Page 69** *Anyone Can Bake* ©1928 Royal Baking Powder Co. **Page 70** *The Young Folks' Cook Book* ©1946 Harriet and Laurence Lustig, The Citadel Press, New York. **Page 72** *Grow Thin on Good Food* by Luella E. Axtell, M.D. ©1930 Funk & Wagnalls Co., New York. **Pages 74–75** *Magic Menus with Mueller's* © 1937 C. F. Mueller Co., Jersey City, NJ. **Page 76** *Cookies Galore* ©1956 General FoodsCorporation. **Page 78** *Party Book* ©1937 The Saalfield Publishing Company, Akron, OH. **Page 80** *Bettina's Cakes and Cookies* by Louise Bennett Weaver and Helen Cowles LeCron ©1924 A. L. Burt Publishers, New York. **Page 82** *Cooking is Fun* by Juliet Scott Miller ©1938 Whitman Publishing Co., Racine, Wisconsin. **Page 84** *The Presto Recipe Book for Little Girls and their Mothers* ©1939 Hecker Products Corporation. **Page 86** *Mary Alden's Cook Book for Children,* An R. H. Loeb Recipix Book, Pictures by Dorothy King ©1955 Wonder Books, Inc. **Page 88** *The New Basic Cookbook* ©1947, 1956, 1961 by Marjorie M. Heseltine and Ula Dow Keezer. Published by Houghton Mifflin Co., Boston. **Page 90** W. B. Roddenbery Co, Cairo, GA. **Page 92** *Mary Alden's Cake and Cookie Cook Book for Children* ©1956 Wonder Books, New York. **Page 94** *Women's Institue of Library Cookery* ©1925 Women's Institue of Domestic Arts and Sciences, Inc., Scranton, PA. **Page 96** *The Wonderful Cookie and Other Stories* ©1899 The Werner Company, Akron OH. **Pages 98–99** *Household Arts for Home and School,* Vol. II by Anna M. Cooley and Wilhelmina H. Spohr ©1920 The Macmillan Company, New York. **Page 100** *Friends: A Primer* ©1929 by Mary E. Pennell and Alice M. Cusack, Published by Ginn and Company. **Page 102** *Jack O'Lantern* © Ferry-Morse Seed Company, Inc., Fulton, KY. **Page 104** *121 Good Things to Eat* ©1940 Chr. Hansen's Laboratory, Inc. Little Falls, NJ, Salada Foods. **Pages 106–107** *Household Arts for Home and School,* Vol. II by Anna M. Cooley and Wilhelmina H. Spohr ©1920 The Macmillan Compamy, New York. **Pages 108–109** *Child Life Cookbook* by Clara Ingram Judson ©1926 RandMcNally, New York. **Page 110** *Mon Premier Livre de Francais* ©1954 Librairie Delagrave, Paris. **Page 112** *Food & Fun for Daughter and Son* by Lila W. Erminger and Marjorie R. Hopkins © 1947 The Illinois Children's home and Aid Society, Chicago, IL. **Pages 114–115** *Storyland Cook Book* by Helen Jill Fletcher and Jack Deckter, Illustrations by Dorcas ©1948 by Helen Jill Fletcher and Jack Deckter. **Pages 116–117** *A Child's First Cook Book* by Alma S. Lach, Illustrations by Doris Stolberg. **Page 118** *Let's Start Cooking* by Garel Clark, Illustrations by Kathleen Elgin ©1961 William R. Scott, Inc., New York. **Page 119** *The Young Folks' Cook Book* ©1946 Harriet and Laurence Lustig, The Citadel Press, New York. **Page 120** Illustrators unknown. **Page 122–123** *Mary Alden's Cake and Cookie Cook Book for Children* ©1956 Wonder Books, New York. **Page 124** *Food & Fun for Daughter and Son* by Lila W. Erminger and Marjorie R. Hopkins ©1947 The Illinois Children's Home and Aid Society, Chicago. **Pages 126–127** *Let's Start Cooking* by Garel Clark, Illustrations by Kathleen Elgin ©1961 William R. Scott, Inc., New York. **Page 128** *Grow Thin on Good Food* by Luella E. Axtell, M.D. ©1930 Funk & Wagnalls Co., New York. **Page 129** *Things to Cook* by Helen Jill Fletcher ©1951 Paxton-Slade Publishing, New York. **Page 130** *Electric Refrigerator Menus and Recipes* by Miss Alice Bradley ©1927 General Electric Company, Cleveland, Ohio. **Page 132–133** Publisher Unknown. **Page 134** *Helping Mother* ©1940 Samuel Gabriel Sons & Co., New York. **Page 136** Publisher unknown **Page 137** *Junior Jewish Cook Book* by Aunt Fanny ©1956 Ktav Publishing House Drawings by Cyla London. **Pages 138–139** *Women's Home Companion Cook Book* ©1942, 1943, 1944, 1945, 1946 by P. F. Collier & Sons Corporation. **Page 140** *Cooking is Fun* by Juliet Scott Miller ©1938 Whitman Publishing Co., Racine, Wisconsin. **Page 141** Publisher unknown. **Pages 142–145** *Storyland Cook Book* by Helen Jill Fletcher and Jack Deckter, Illustrations by Dorcas ©1948 by Helen Jill Fletcher and Jack Deckter. **Page 146** *Cooking is Fun* by Juliet Scott Miller ©1938 Whitman Publishing, Racine, Wisconsin. **Endpapers** *Learning to Cook and Serve Our Meals* by Ada R. Polkinghorne ©1946 National Dairy Council, Chicago. **Back Cover** *Helping Mother* ©1940 Samuel Gabriel & Sons NY

loaf

woode

wire cake t

saucepan

sciss

waffle iron

cake pan

paring knife

candy thermometer

sieve

slotted spoon

ACKNOWLEDGMENTS

I would like to thank the following people for their help and encouragement: Claire Calmettes, Diana Edkins, Bea Feitler, Sallie Gouverneur, Mariah Hughs, Beth Huseman, Andrea Meislin, Amy Newman, Barbara Richer, Nancy Rosen, Ruth Sorenson, Daniel and Lily Snyder (the two best buns from my oven), James Snyder (impeccable taster), Leslie Stoker (who went the extra mile), Bradbury Thompson, and Linda Zisquit. Extra special thanks to my mother, Bernice Sapirstein Davis. Clearly, I had a very happy childhood.